MILITARY MISSIONS

RECON

BY NEL YOMTOV

EPIC

BELLWETHER MEDIA • MINNEAPOLIS, MN

EPIC BOOKS are no ordinary books. They burst with intense action, high-speed heroics, and shadows of the unknown. Are you ready for an Epic adventure?

This edition first published in 2017 by Bellwether Media, Inc.

No part of this publication may be reproduced in whole or in part without written permission of the publisher.
For information regarding permission, write to Bellwether Media, Inc., Attention: Permissions Department, 5357 Penn Avenue South, Minneapolis, MN 55419.

Library of Congress Cataloging-in-Publication Data

Names: Yomtov, Nelson, author.
Title: Recon / by Nel Yomtov.
Description: Minneapolis, MN : Bellwether Media, Inc., 2017. | Series: Epic:
  Military Missions | Includes bibliographical references and index. |
  Audience: Grades 2-7.
Identifiers: LCCN 2016004365 | ISBN 9781626174375 (hardcover
: alk. paper)
Subjects: LCSH: United States. Marine Corps. Force Reconnaissance–
Juvenile literature. | United States. Marine Corps–Commando troops–
Juvenile literature.
Classification: LCC VE23 .Y66 2017 | DDC 359.9/64130973–dc23
LC record available at http://lccn.loc.gov/2016004365

Printed in the United States of America, North Mankato, MN.

TABLE OF CONTENTS

JUNGLE ATTACK!

Enemy troops hide in the forest in Vietnam. A United States Marine **Force Recon** team heads out to find them.

The Marines search the jungle. Finally, they find the enemy.

CHINA

LAOS

THAILAND

VIETNAM

CAMBODIA

N
W · E
S

EARLY RECON

The first Marine Force Recon team formed in 1957.

5

The Marines call their **commander**. They give the enemy's location. Within minutes, American aircraft arrive.

The aircraft attack with rockets. Soon, the enemy runs off. The Marines have done their job!

THE MISSION

Recon soldiers gather **intelligence**. This helps the military decide when and how to strike.

Small recon teams watch enemies' movements. They learn about enemy weapons and **territory**.

HAND TALK

Recon teams move silently. They use hand signals to share information with one another.

Recon troops travel with as few supplies as possible. This helps them move quickly and quietly.

They are prepared for anything. If they meet the enemy, they are armed to fight.

REAL-LIFE RECON

What: Recon mission in Guam

Who: United States Army, 77th Reconnaissance Troop

Where: Guam, Pacific Ocean

When: July 28-August 2, 1944, during World War II

Why: Gather intelligence about the Japanese military

How: U.S. troops patrolled southern Guam for enemy troops; used the intelligence gained to defeat the Japanese military in Guam.

United States Marines advance on Japanese positions in Guam, 1944

THE PLAN

Some recon teams work near the main Army units. They may also go deep into enemy lands.

NEVER GIVE UP

Marine Force Recon teams are tough. One of their beliefs is "I shall never quit."

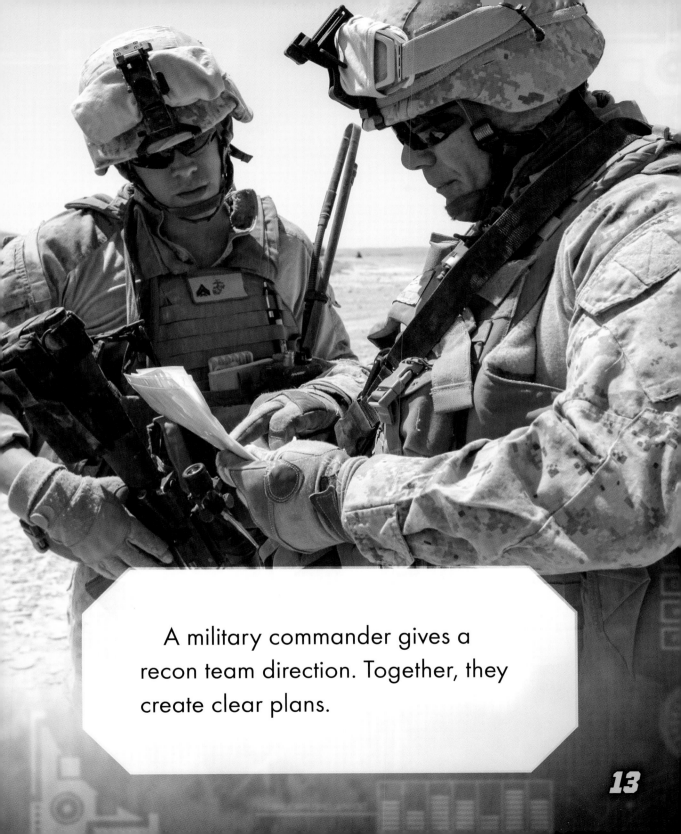

A military commander gives a recon team direction. Together, they create clear plans.

Soldiers can do recon in or near the water. They may swim or use small boats.

Sometimes recon troops **parachute** from planes. They also complete missions on foot.

RECON EQUIPMENT AND GEAR

M9 pistol

M240 machine gun

M4 carbine

LAV (light armored vehicle)

UH-1H Huey helicopter

KC-130 Super Hercules

THE TEAM

Each branch of the U.S. military uses recon teams. Often the teams are part of **Special Operations**. Some of these teams are trained for **raids**. They may also rescue **hostages**.

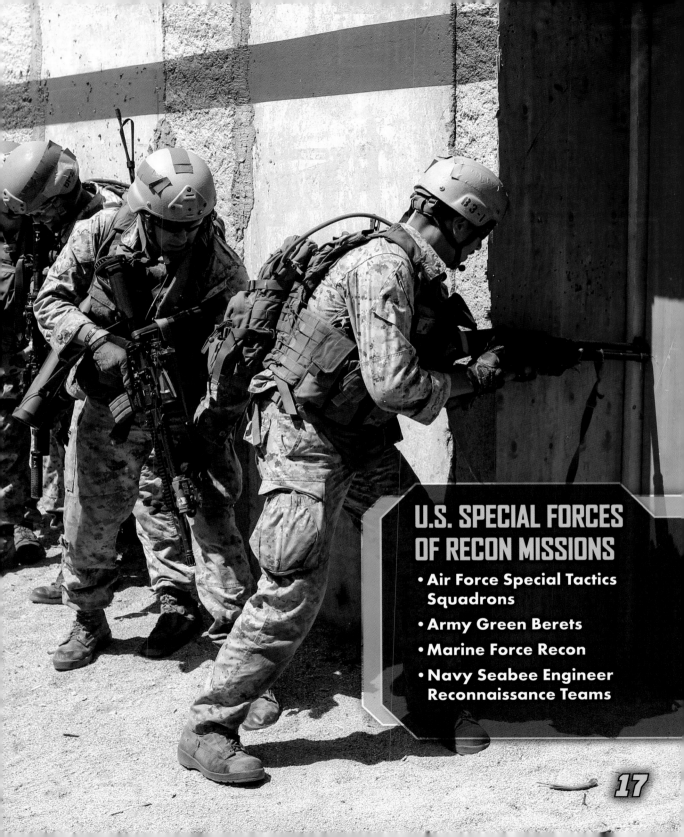

U.S. SPECIAL FORCES OF RECON MISSIONS

- Air Force Special Tactics Squadrons
- Army Green Berets
- Marine Force Recon
- Navy Seabee Engineer Reconnaissance Teams

Recon requires special training and skills. Soldiers learn how to avoid capture by the enemy.

Many are good swimmers and can run fast. They also practice moving in the dark at night.

ACCOMPLISHED!

The most successful recon missions end without violence. The goal is to gather information in secret. This helps the military win battles!

GLOSSARY

commander—a leader of a group who is often a military officer

Force Recon—a specialized group of United States Marines that completes recon missions; recon is short for reconnaissance.

hostages—people who are captured by a person or group that wants something in exchange for their freedom

intelligence—information about an enemy's position, movements, or weapons

parachute—to jump from an aircraft with a parachute; a parachute is a large, umbrella-shaped cloth attached to someone to help them fall safely from the air.

raids—surprise attacks

Special Operations—military missions carried out by specially trained forces that use uncommon practices

territory—an area of land owned by a group or a government

TO LEARN MORE

AT THE LIBRARY

Gordon, Nick. *Marine Corps Force Recon*. Minneapolis, Minn.: Bellwether Media, 2013.

Lüsted, Marcia Amidon. *Marine Force Recon: Elite Operations*. Minneapolis, Minn.: Lerner Publications, 2014.

Newman, Patricia. *Navy SEALs: Elite Operations*. Minneapolis, Minn.: Lerner Publications, 2014.

ON THE WEB

Learning more about recon is as easy as 1, 2, 3.

1. Go to www.factsurfer.com.

2. Enter "recon" into the search box.

3. Click the "Surf" button and you will see a list of related web sites.

With factsurfer.com, finding more information is just a click away.

INDEX

The images in this book are reproduced through the courtesy of: United States Department of Defense/ DVIDS, front cover (left, top right), pp. 8-9, 9, 10, 11, 12, 12-13, 14, 14 (top), 15 (LAV, UH-1H Huey helicopter), 16-17, 18, 18 (top), 19, 20, 21; A_Lesik, front cover (bottom right); MILpictures by Tom Weber/ Getty Images, pp. 4-5, 6-7; Larry Burrows/ Getty Images, p. 7; United States Department of Defense/ United States Marine Corps History Division, p. 11 (top); Jaroslaw Grudzinski, p. 15 (M9 handgun); Militarist, p. 15 (M4 carbine); United States Department of Defense/ Wikipedia, p. 15 (M240 machine gun, KC-130 Super Hercules).